NCERT PRACTICE WORK BOOK

ENGLISH

MARIGOLD

Emmanuel D'Souza
Gloria D'Souza

ARIHANT PRAKASHAN, MEERUT

WORKBOOK English 2nd

Published by Arihant Prakashan, Meerut

Administrative & Production Offices

Regd. Office
'Ramchhaya' 4577/15, Agarwal Road, Darya Ganj, New Delhi -110002
Tele: 011- 47630600, 43518550; Fax: 011- 23280316

Head Office
Kalindi, TP Nagar, Meerut (UP) - 250002
Tel: 0121-2401479, 2512970, 4004199; Fax: 0121-2401648

Sales & Support Offices

Agra, Ahmedabad, Bengaluru, Bhubaneswar, Bareilly, Chennai, Delhi, Guwahati, Hyderabad, Jaipur, Jhansi, Kolkata, Lucknow, Meerut, Nagpur & Pune.

ISBN 978-93-11122-07-6

Price ₹ 80.00

For further information about the books published by Arihant, log on to **www.arihantbooks.com** or e-mail at **info@arihantbooks.com**

Production Team

Publishing Managers
Keshav Mohan, Amit Verma

Project Head
Karishma Yadav

Project Coordinator
Aleena Zaidi

Project Editor
Mridula Sharma

Cover Designer
Shanu Mansoori

Inner Designer
Ravi Negi

Proof Readers
Esha, Soniya

Workbook, Why?

"Knowledge will not be with you for Long Unless You Practice"

This quotation answer the above question 'Workbook, Why ?' perfectly i.e. Workbooks are made to give the students practice required to achieve perfection and mastery in the subject. These are the only Workbooks, which are strictly based on **NCERT, the only recommended books by Govt. of India & CBSE** (reference Circular No. Acad-41/2015 dated 20th July 2015).

Given below is the detailed description of Workbook and some of its special features

ONLY COMPLETE WORKBOOK BASED ON NCERT

NCERT textbooks are the only textbooks, which have been prepared according to National Curriculum Framework, which discourages the idea of rote learning rather focus on inculcating creativity & initiative in the students to make them participants in learning not just a receiver of a one-way communication.

Keeping the importance of NCERT textbooks in mind we have prepared this Workbook, strictly based on NCERT content, this Workbook will complement NCERT by providing practice on the material given in each chapter of NCERT textbook. This is the only Workbook, which covers complete Syllabus of English.

WORKBOOK- PURPOSE, USE & FEATURES

This Workbook, through its **numerous exercises** having different **variety of questions** covering **practical importance** of English & **Day-to-Day communication**, will prove to be **equally useful** for both, **Classroom** and **at Home**. One more purpose of this Workbook is to provide the students a **systematic practice** of the content taught in the class and what they study in the textbooks.

Some special features of this Workbook are

- Complete coverage of all the Sections; Literature, Grammar and Writing
- Complete coverage of all the Chapters of the NCERT Textbook
- Different variety of questions; Fill in the Blanks, True-False, Matching, Multiple Choice Questions, Very Short Answer, Short Answer etc.

WORKBOOK-DESIGNED TO IMPROVE SUBJECT ABILITIES

All the material given in this Workbook is tailored to suit subject content with equal support on learning, which will surely help students to boost their abilities and confidence in the subject.

I look forward for the feedback from students, teachers and parents for the further improvement of the contents of this book. I will try to update the contents according to your feedback in further editions of this Workbook.

The Publisher

Contents

SECTION A Literature

SECTION B Grammar

SECTION C Writing Skills

01

First Day at School

Text Based Questions

1. Tick (✓) the correct option.

(i) This poem is about __________ before he goes to school on the first day.

(a) what a child thinks ☐ (b) experiences of a child ☐

(c) a wonderful child ☐ (d) None of these ☐

(ii) The child wonders about this teacher will look like __________.

(a) puppy ☐ (b) mom or gran ☐

(c) friends ☐ (d) neighbour ☐

(iii) The child's pet is a __________ .

(a) kitten ☐ (b) parrot ☐

(c) puppy ☐ (d) frog ☐

2. Answer the following questions

(i) When you entered your class what did you like?

____

(ii) Who was the first friend you made?

____

(iii) How did you feel when you went to school first day?

____

(iv) Do you think the child would like to carry his puppy to school?

____

Language Based Questions

3. Complete the opposites of the following words.

(i) Day N __ __ h __

(ii) Friend E __ e __ __

(iii) Full __ m p __ __

(iv) Good B __ __

(v) Laugh C __ __

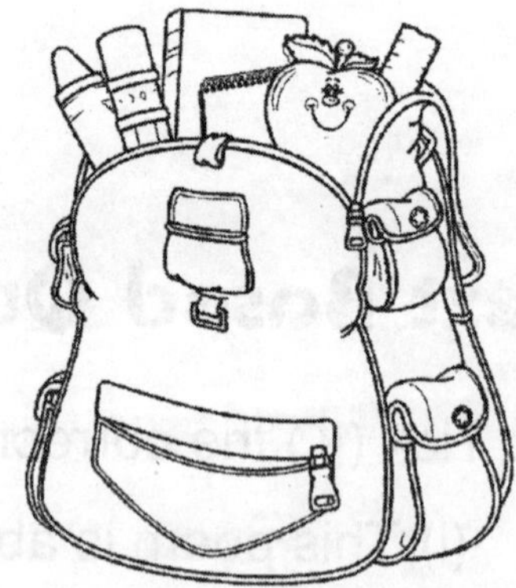

4. Manjula is a class II student. Her teacher found the items given below in Manjula's bag. Decide if they should be in her schoolbag or not. Circle Yes or No.

S. No.	Items found	Should be in bag?	
(i)	Sharpener	Yes	No
(ii)	Water bottle	Yes	No
(iii)	Doll	Yes	No
(iv)	Eraser	Yes	No
(v)	Toy aeroplane	Yes	No
(vi)	Tiffin	Yes	No

5. See the picture given below and answer the questions based on it.

(i) What is the thing marked as A?

(ii) Who is the person marked B?

(iii) Who are the persons marked C?

02

Haldi's Adventure

Text Based Questions

1. Tick (✓) the correct option.

(i) Haldi was going ________ .

(a) to the hospital ☐ (b) home ☐

(c) to the market ☐ (d) to school ☐

(ii) The giraffe was named ________ .

(a) Giraffe ☐ (b) Haldi ☐

(c) Smiley ☐ (d) None of these ☐

(iii) Haldi had a ________ by riding on Smiley's back.

(a) good time ☐ (b) headache ☐

(c) wonderful adventure ☐ (d) difficult time ☐

2. State 'T' for True and 'F' for False statements.

(i) Haldi was surprised, but happy to meet Smiley. ☐

(ii) Smiley wore blue coloured glasses. ☐

(iii) The giraffe had a wonderful adventure. ☐

(iv) Haldi climbed on Smiley's long neck. ☐

(v) Haldi ran fast to reach school on time. ☐

3. Match the pictures in Column A with what they are about in Column B.

Column A	Column B
(i)	(a) Haldi riding on Smiley
(ii)	(b) Feeding the birds
(iii)	(c) Smiley talking to Haldi
(iv)	(d) Playing at the paddling pool
(v)	(e) Ringing bells

4. Fill in the blanks in the part of the story which is given below.

Mondays, Thursdays, Fridays, school, giraffe, school, day, play, games, school

(i) Do you go to ________ every ________?"

(ii) "Yes," said Haldi. "I go to school on ________, Tuesdays,

Wednesdays, ________ and ________ .

(iii) On Saturdays I ________, ________ at ________."

(iv) "What do you do in ________?" asked the ________.

5. Read the parts of the story given below and answer the following questions.

So she said to the giraffe, "I would love to talk to you but I must rush to school or I will be late." The giraffe said, "Not if you ride on my back. If you climb on my back, I will run so fast that you will feel you are flying to school."

(i) Why could Haldi not wait and talk to the giraffe?

____

(ii) How did she reach school?

____

(iii) Write the opposite of the word 'fast'.

____

6. On the basis of the chapter give answers to the following questions.

(i) When Haldi met Smiley, what did he have in his hand? (Book/Newspaper/Toys)

____

(ii) What was Smiley wearing on his face? (Mask/Big Glasses/Cap)

____

(iii) What does Haldi learn in school? Choose from the given words and write them. (Stars/Birds/Trees/Animals/Colours/Games/Dance)

(iv) On which day Haldi play games? (Saturdays/Sundays/Mondays)

(v) Where was the giraffe, when Haldi turned back to him? (Playground/Gone Away/School)

Language Based Questions

7. Make a sentence of your own using each of the given words.

(i) Adventure

(ii) Giraffe

(iii) Playground

(iv) Surprised

(v) Wonderful

01

I am Lucky

Text Based Questions

1. Tick (✓) the correct option.

(i) The butterfly is thankful for ________ .

(a) its eight arms ☐ (b) being able to fly ☐

(c) its wings ☐ (d) All of these ☐

(ii) The myna is thankful to be able to ________ .

(a) hop ☐ (b) sing ☐

(c) fly ☐ (d) giggle ☐

2. State 'T' for True and 'F' for False statements.

(i) The kangaroo would try to hop to the Moon. ☐

(ii) The octopus is thankful for its four legs. ☐

(iii) The fish is thankful for being able to read. ☐

(iv) The elephant is thankful to raise its trunk. ☐

3. Complete the following lines of the poem with the suitable words given in the brackets.

(i) If I ___________ an elephant. (were/was)

(ii) I would be ___________. (thankless/thankful)

(iii) That I can ___________ my ___________. (fall/raise, tail/trunk)

(iv) If I were a ___________. (kangaroo/lion)

(v) I would ___________ to hop. (run/try)

(vi) Right up to the ___________. (sun/moon)

4. Match the pictures in Column A with what they are about in Column B by drawing lines.

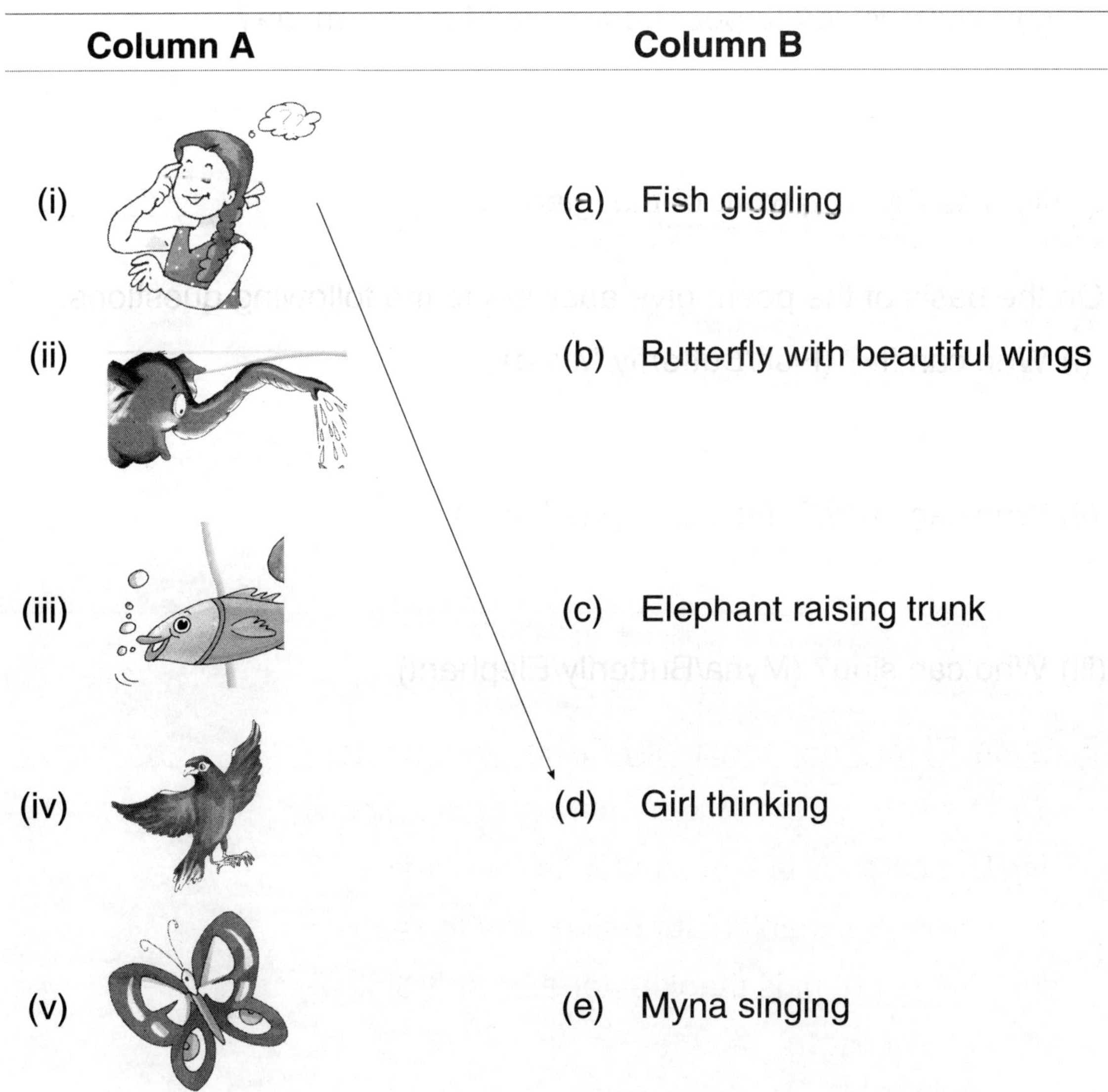

Column A	Column B
(i)	(a) Fish giggling
(ii)	(b) Butterfly with beautiful wings
(iii)	(c) Elephant raising trunk
(iv)	(d) Girl thinking
(v)	(e) Myna singing

5. Read the following lines of the poem and answer the questions that follow.

If I were a myna in a tree
I would be thankful
That I could sing.
If I were a fish in the sea
I would be thankful
That I can wriggle and giggle with glee.

(i) What two wishes are given in the above lines?

____

(ii) What would the poet be thankful for as a myna?

____

(iii) The rhyming word of the 'glee' is ______________.

6. On the basis of the poem give answers to the following questions.

(i) Who can fly? (Fish/Butterfly/Myna)

____

(ii) Who can swim? (Fish/Octopus/Myna)

____

(iii) Who can sing? (Myna/Butterfly/Elephant)

____

Language Based Questions

7. Choose the correct antonym/opposite word from the box given below.

Drop, Thankless, Cry, Unhappiness

(i) Thankful ____________ (ii) Giggle ____________

(iii) Glee ____________ (iv) Raise ____________

8. Write the plural of the following words.

(i) Butterfly ____________ (ii) Fish ____________

(iii) Trunk ____________ (iv) Moon ____________

(v) Octopus ____________

9. The following words have been taken from the poem and are jumbled. Rearrange them properly.

(i) HATNKUFL ____________

(ii) RETE ____________

(iii) GILGEG ____________

(iv) AIRSE ____________

(v) GHIRT ____________

02

I Want

Text Based Questions

1. Tick (✓) the correct option.

(i) The monkey wanted to be ________ .

(a) tall and slim ☐ (b) big and strong ☐

(c) short and fat ☐ (d) small and thin ☐

(ii) The monkey's first wish was to have ________ .

(a) long tail ☐ (b) human body ☐

(c) long neck ☐ (d) beautiful face ☐

(iii) Next the monkey wished to ________ .

(a) fill his trunk with water ☐ (b) fill his mouth with sand ☐

(c) play in mud ☐ (d) fill his mouth with sugar ☐

2. State 'T' for True and 'F' for False statements.

(i) The wise woman gave the monkey a magic wand. ☐

(ii) The monkey did not want to have a trunk like an elephant. ☐

(iii) The monkey threw away the magic wand in the water. ☐

(iv) A wise woman does not hear him. ☐

3. Read the lines of the story and answer the questions.

A wise woman hears him. "Take this magic wand", she says, "and all your wishes can come true." A giraffe comes by. He stretches his long neck. He eats the sweet leaves at the top of the trees.

(i) Who gave the monkey a magic wand?

....

(ii) Who can stretches his long neck?

....

(iii) The meaning of the word 'hear' is __________ .

4. On the basis of the poem give answers to the following questions.

(i) Who hears the monkey? (Wise Woman/Giraffe)

(ii) What does the wise woman give the monkey? (Magic Wand/Coins)

(iii) What does the monkey wish for when he sees a giraffe? (Long Tail/Long Neck)

(iv) Whose stripes did the monkey want for himself? (Zebra/Elephant)

(v) What does the zebra have? (Spots/Stripes)

Language Based Questions

5. Match Column A with Column B to complete the sentences.

	Column A		Column B
(i)	A giraffe comes by	(a)	just like the zebra.
(ii)	An elephant comes to the river	(b)	himself in the water.
(iii)	Little monkey has stripes all over his body	(c)	and he jumps with joy.
(iv)	The monkey sees	(d)	and stretches his long neck.
(v)	Little monkey is himself again	(e)	to fill his trunk with water.

6. Choose the correct spelling from the options given below.

(i) (a) Aewful ☐ (b) Aweful ☐
(c) Awful ☐ (d) Auful ☐

(ii) (a) Wheiz ☐ (b) Whizz ☐
(c) Weehz ☐ (d) Wihze ☐

(iii) (a) Megik ☐ (b) Maagic ☐
(c) Meigic ☐ (d) Magic ☐

(iv) (a) Monster ☐ (b) Maunster ☐
(c) Moonstre ☐ (d) Mawnster ☐

(v) (a) Streips ☐ (b) Stripees ☐
(c) Estrips ☐ (d) Stripes ☐

7. Write the names of the animals shown in the pictures below.

(i) ____________________

(ii) ____________________

(iii) ____________________

(iv) ____________________

01

A Smile

Text Based Questions

1. Tick (✓) the correct option.

(i) This poem tells the importance of ________ .

(a) being happy ☐ (b) being funny ☐

(c) making faces ☐ (d) having a smile on your face ☐

(ii) Where does smile go away?

(a) We can find it anywhere ☐

(b) It goes and comes turnwise ☐

(c) It goes to a secret hiding place ☐

(d) Smile never disappears ☐

(iii) A smile is always good as

(a) it keeps us fresh ☐

(b) it makes the other person smile ☐

(c) it makes everybody laugh loudly ☐

(d) it energises us ☐

2. State 'T' for True and 'F' for False statements.

(i) A smile can wrinkle your face. ☐

(ii) A smile goes away fast. ☐

(iii) Smiling is an irritating action. ☐

(iv) A smile brings smile on other's faces also. ☐

(v) Smile does not make one into two. ☐

3. Fill in the blanks and complete the poem with the suitable words given in the box.

secret, smiles, funny, wonderful

(i) Smile is a ______________ thing.

(ii) One cannot find smile's ______________ hiding place.

(iii) It is ______________ to see what smile can do.

(iv) You smile at one, he ______________ at you.

4. Complete the following words.

(i) WRI____KLE

(ii) NE____ER

(iii) SM____LE

(iv) FUN____Y

(v) WON____ER

Language Based Questions

5. Match words in Column A with their rhyming words in Column B.

	Column A		Column B
(i)	Thing	(a)	Man
(ii)	Face	(b)	To
(iii)	But	(c)	Sing
(iv)	Can	(d)	Cut
(v)	Do	(e)	Race

6. Write the meaning of the words given below.

(i) Wonderful ______ (ii) Hide ______

(iii) Far ______ (iv) See ______

7. Draw smileys in the given circle.

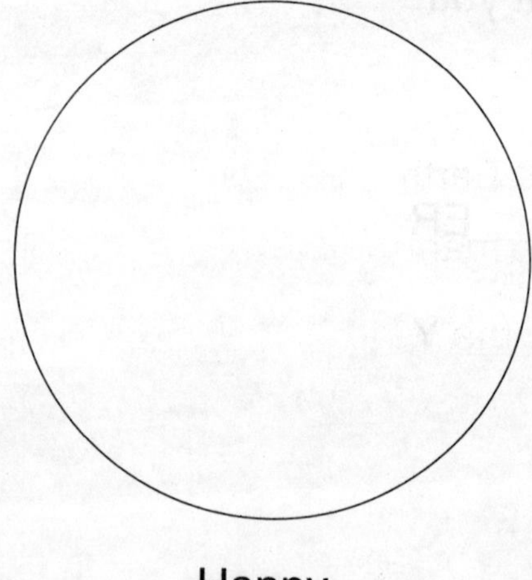

Happy

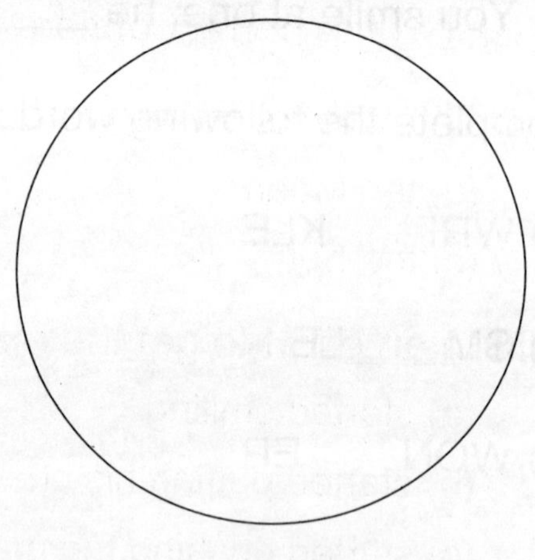

Sad

02

The Wind and the Sun

Text Based Questions

1. Tick (✓) the correct option.

(i) The wind is talking to ________ .

(a) the Moon ☐ (b) the Earth ☐

(c) the Sun ☐ (d) the man ☐

(ii) In an effort to get the man's coat off, the wind ________ .

(a) started smiling ☐

(b) started puffing his cheeks ☐

(c) started pushing the man ☐

(d) started blowing harder and harder ☐

(iii) The man decided to take off his coat because ________ .

(a) there were ants in his coat ☐

(b) there was dust in his coat ☐

(c) the man was not comfortable in his coat ☐

(d) the man was feeling hot in his coat ☐

2. State 'T' for True and 'F' for False statements.

(i) A man was running on the road. ☐

(ii) The Sun allows the wind to try first to take off the man's coat. ☐

(iii) The Sun shone very brightly. ☐

(iv) The Wind made the man take off his coat. ☐

3. Read the extract given below and answer the questions that follow.

Man : How strong the wind is today ! It is blowing my coat away ! I must hold it tightly around myself.

Wind (blowing harder) : Whoooooh ...... Whooooo !

Man (pulling his coat more tightly) : How cold it is !

Wind : Sun, I give up. I cannot get his coat off !

Sun : Now it is my turn. Let me try. (He shines hard)

(i) How does the man feel about the wind ?

____

(ii) Who said, "Now it is my trun. Let me try?"

____

(iii) Write the rhyming word of 'cold'.

____

4. On the basis of the chapter give answers to the following questions.

(i) Where did the wind see the man? (Park/Road/Home)

____

(ii) Who offered to get the man's coat off? (Moon/Sun/Wind)

____

(iii) What did the wind do to win? (Stop/Blowing Harder/Smile)

____

(iv) What did the man do to save his coat? (Hold Tightly/Put Off/Loose)

____

(v) What did the Sun try to do? (Blow Hard/Shines Hard)

____

(vi) Who was stronger? (Sun/Wind/Man)

____

Language Based Questions

5. Fill in the blanks by choosing right word from the box given below.

away, won, that, turn, cannot

(i) Can you see ________ man?

(ii) It is blowing my coat ________ !

(iii) I ________ get his coat off.

(iv) Now it is my ________ .

(v) Wind, I have ________ .

6. Rearrange the words given below to make a meaningful sentence.

(i) me/let/try. ____________________

(ii) stronger/is/who? ____________________

(iii) hard/he/shines. ____________________

(iv) up/I/give. ____________________

7. There are many things in the picture. Write the names of any five in the blank space given below.

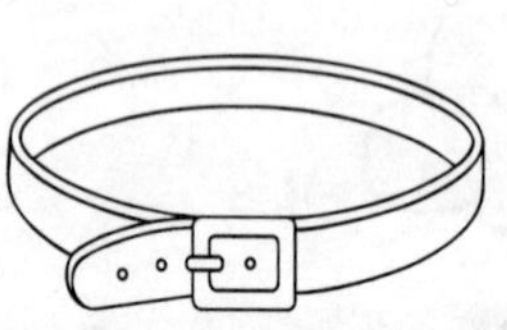
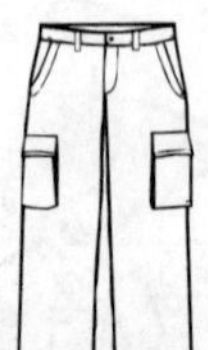

(i) ____________________

(ii) ____________________

(iii) ____________________

(iv) ____________________

(v) ____________________

(vi) ____________________

01 Rain

Text Based Questions

1. Tick (✓) the correct option.

(i) In this poem it did not rain on the ________ .

(a) trees ☐ (b) umbrellas ☐

(c) ships ☐ (d) girl ☐

(ii) The term 'all around' used in this poem refers to ________ .

(a) sea ☐ (b) round objects ☐

(c) everywhere ☐ (d) field and tree ☐

(iii) People use ________ when it rains.

(a) trees ☐ (b) field ☐

(c) umbrellas ☐ (d) ships ☐

2. State 'T' for True and 'F' for False statements.

(i) It is not raining. ☐

(ii) It is raining heavily. ☐

(iii) The rain is falling on the field and the trees. ☐

3. Fill in the blanks and complete the poem with the suitable words given in the box.

umbrellas, field, sea, raining

(i) The rain is __________ all around.

(ii) It falls on __________ and tree.

(iii) It rains on the __________ here.

(iv) And on the ships at the __________.

4. Read the lines given below and answer the questions that follow.

It rains on the umbrellas here
And on the ships at sea.

(i) Name the things on which it rains in the above lines.

____

(ii) What do people use when it rains?

____

(iii) Do you like to play in rain? Yes or No.

____

5. On the basis of the poem give answers to the following questions.

(i) Where does the rain fall in the poem? (Field/People/Water)

____

(ii) What things live in water? (Ships/Umbrellas/Peoples)

____

(iii) How do children protect themselves from the rain? (Ships/Field/Umbrellas)

____

Language Based Questions

6. Write one word in each box that rhymes with the one mentioned in it.

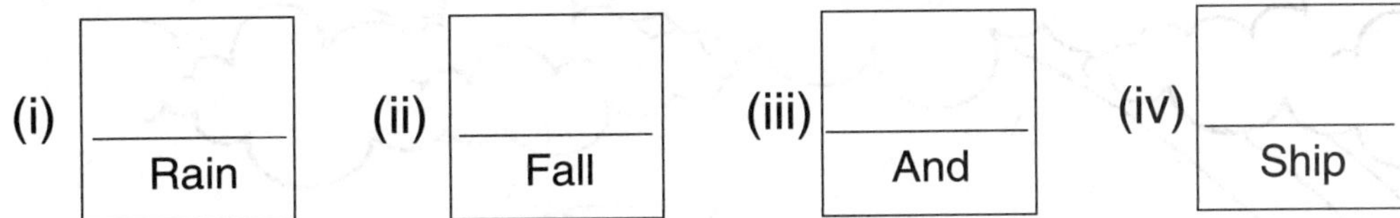

7. Circle the odd word.

(i) Rain	Wind	Lightning	Duck
(ii) Ship	Boat	Engine	Steamer
(iii) Rainbow	Cloud	Thunder	Sea
(iv) Umbrella	Raincoat	Rain-boot	Socks

8. Write the plural of the following words.

(i) Field ____________________

(ii) Tree ____________________

(iii) Ship ____________________

(iv) Sea ____________________

9. The words mentioned below are formed by joining two words. Complete them. One has been done for you.

(i) Rain + Fall   Rainfall

(ii) Sun + Shine ____________

(iii) Moon + Light ____________

(iv) Cloud + Burst ____________

(v) Week + End ____________

(vi) Rain + Bow ____________

10. Write five sentences based on the picture given below.

(i) ____________________

(ii) ____________________

(iii) ____________________

(iv) ____________________

(v) ____________________

02

Storm in the Garden

Text Based Questions

1. Tick (✓) the correct option.

(i) The snail was visiting his ________ .

(a) enemies ☐ (b) relatives ☐

(c) parents ☐ (d) friends ☐

(ii) A great white light crashed through the ________ .

(a) garden ☐ (b) clouds ☐

(c) tree ☐ (d) flower pot ☐

(iii) The crow made the noise as ________ .

(a) Shay ! Shay ! Shay ! ☐ (b) Zzzak ! Zzzak ! ☐

(c) Kaa ! Kaa ! Kaa! ☐ (d) Ooo ! Ooo ! Ooo ! ☐

(iv) Sunu-sunu's mother sat under a ________ .

(a) stone ☐ (b) tree ☐

(c) flower pot ☐ (d) cup ☐

2. State 'T' for True and 'F' for False statements.

(i) Sunu-sunu was an ant. ☐

(ii) The ants climbed over Sunu-sunu. ☐

(iii) The sky grew dark and the crows flew past. ☐

(iv) Sunu-sunu got wet in the rain. ☐

3. Read the following lines and answer the questions that follow.

Suddenly a great white light crashed through the clouds. Sunu-sunu quickly pulled in his head, pulled in his tail, and sat very still. Outside, the sky grew dark and the crows flew past. Kaa! Kaa! Kaa!

(i) What happened suddenly?

____

(ii) How did Sunu-sunu react to the white light?

____

(iii) Write the rhyming word of 'quickly'.

____

4. On the basis of the chapter give answers to the following questions.

(i) Where was Sunu-sunu going? (Friends/Home/Market)

____

(ii) Who were Sunu-sunus' friends? (Ants/Crows/Trees)

____

(iii) Who was under the flower pot? (Feelers/Storm/Ants)

____

(iv) Who was Sunu-sunu? (Snail/Ant/Crow)

____

Language Based Questions

5. Write the opposites of the following words.

(i) Pull _______________ (ii) Light _______________

(iii) Wet _______________ (iv) Under _______________

6. Write the names of the following.

(i) _______________ (ii) _______________ (iii) _______________

(iv) _______________ (v) _______________

01

Zoo Manners

1. Tick (✓) the correct option.

(i) The camel is very ________ of his hump.

(a) loud ☐ (b) rude ☐

(c) humble ☐ (d) proud ☐

(ii) Various types of birds and ________ are found in the zoo.

(a) jokers ☐ (b) animals ☐

(c) bees ☐ (d) cheese ☐

(iii) We should not ________ and feed the animals at the zoo.

(a) tease ☐ (b) see ☐

(c) look ☐ (d) pray ☐

2. State 'T' for True and 'F' for False statements.

(i) We should be careful about what we do when we visit the zoo. ☐

(ii) One should make fun of the camel's hump. ☐

(iii) The chimpanzee thinks that he is foolish. ☐

(iv) The penguins cannot understand our remarks. ☐

(v) We should treat animals with love and affection. ☐

3. Fill in the blanks to complete the parts of the poem with the suitable words given in the brackets.

(i) Be ____________ what you say or do. (careful/careless)

(ii) Don't make ____________ of the camel's hump. (noise/fun)

(iii) Don't laugh too ____________ at the chimpanzee. (less/much)

(iv) The penguins can ____________ remarks you make. (understand/misunderstand)

(v) Treat them as ____________ as they do you. (well/soon)

4. Read the lines given below and answer the questions that follow.

Be careful what
You say or do
When you visit the animals
At the zoo.

(i) What do you see when you visit the zoo?

____

(ii) Write the rhyming word of 'zoo'.

____

(iii) Give the meaning of the word 'careful'.

____

5. On the basis of the poem give answers to the following questions.

(i) What does the camel have on its back? (Hump/Tail/Leg)

____

(ii) What do penguins do around the lake? (Strutting/Dancing/Sleeping)

____

(iii) Have you been to a zoo? (Yes/No)

____

(iv) What do you see at the zoo? (Animals/Birds/Doctors)

____

Language Based Questions

6. Tick the word which is correctly spelled.

	A		B		C	
(i)	Nobel	☐	Noble	☐	Nobal	☐
(ii)	Proud	☐	Proad	☐	Prowd	☐
(iii)	Logh	☐	Luagh	☐	Laugh	☐
(iv)	Remark	☐	Remork	☐	Remarc	☐
(v)	Strotting	☐	Stratting	☐	Strutting	☐

7. Write one word in each box that rhymes with the one mentioned in it.

(i) ______ Hump (ii) ______ Lake (iii) ______ Well (iv) ______ Treat

8. Name the animals and birds given in the poem.

(i) ______________ (ii) ______________

(iii) ______________ (iv) ______________

(v) ______________ (vi) ______________

(vii) ______________ (viii) ______________

02

Funny Bunny

1. Tick (✓) the correct option.

(i) Funny Bunny told Henny Penny that ________ .

(a) he was unwell ☐ (b) the king wanted to meet him ☐

(c) the sky is going to fall ☐ (d) the tree is going to fall ☐

(ii) Lucky Ducky was the name of a ________ .

(a) Rabbit ☐ (b) Goat ☐

(c) Snail ☐ (d) Duck ☐

(iii) The last one to meet Funny Bunny was ________ .

(a) Goosey Poosey ☐ (b) Henny Penny ☐

(c) Woxy Foxy ☐ (d) Cocky Locky ☐

2. State 'T' for True and 'F' for False statements.

(i) A flower fell on Funny Bunny. ☐

(ii) Funny Bunny thought that the sky is going to fall. ☐

(iii) Funny Bunny wanted to tell the milkman about the incident. ☐

(iv) Funny Bunny met Lucky Ducky on the way. ☐

(v) The king met Funny Bunny. ☐

3. Read the following lines from the story and answer the questions.

"The sky is going to fall, they all said.

"We're going to tell the king."

(i) What is falling down?

____

(ii) Where were they all going?

____

(iii) Write the rhyming word of 'fall'.

____

4. On the basis of the chapter give answers to the following questions.

(i) Where was Funny Bunny sitting one day? (Tree/River/Road)

____

(ii) Who fell on Funny Bunny one day? (Fruit/Mango/Nut)

____

(iii) Who said, "King lives here?" (Funny Bunny/Lucky Ducky/Woxy Foxy)

____

(iv) What is going to fall? (Nut/Sky/Tree)

____

Language Based Questions

5. Expand the following.

(i) I'm ______________ (ii) I'll ______________

(iii) We're ______________

6. Match the following words in Column A with their opposites in Column B.

Column A	Column B
(i) Off	(a) Lost
(ii) End	(b) On
(iii) King	(c) Start
(iv) Found	(d) Queen

7. Find the odd one out from the following.

(i) Red, Green, Blue, Sky, Yellow

(ii) Met, Wet, Gate, Bet, Jet

(iii) Sun, Moon, Ship, Stars, Sky

(iv) Rabbit, Stone, Hen, Cock, Duck

8. Name the following animals from the story.

Unit 6

01

Mr. Nobody

Text Based Questions

1. Tick (✓) the correct option.

(i) Mr. Nobody is ________ .

(a) funny ☐ (b) big ☐

(c) little ☐ (d) funny and little ☐

(ii) Mr. Nobody is as quiet as a ________ .

(a) crocodile ☐ (b) shy man ☐

(c) mouse ☐ (d) house ☐

(iii) Nobody creates mischief apart from ________ .

(a) Mr. Everybody ☐ (b) Mr. Nobody ☐

(c) Mr. Anybody ☐ (d) Children ☐

(iv) All ________ that every plate was broken by Mr. Nobody.

(a) agree ☐ (b) disagree ☐

(c) away ☐ (d) pray ☐

2. Fill in the blanks to complete the poem with the suitable words given in box.

mouse, everybody's, funny, mischief, quiet

I know a (i) __________ little man as (ii) __________ as a (iii) __________, who does the (iv) __________ that is done in (v) __________ house.

3. Read the stanza given below and answer the questions that follow.

There's no one ever sees his face,
And yet we all agree
That every plate we break was cracked
By Mr. Nobody.

(i) What has no one ever seen?

____

(ii) Who crack all the plates?

____

(iii) Write the meaning of the word 'sees' as used in the passage.

____

4. On the basis of the poem give answers to the following questions.

(i) Who is Mr. Nobody? (Strong Man/Big Man/Little Man)

____

(ii) Is these a Mr. Nobody in your house? (Yes/No)

____

(iii) With whom does the poet compare Mr. Nobody? (Mouse/Cat/Rabbit)

____

(iv) Who does mischief in the house? (Child/Mouse/Friend)

____

Language Based Questions

5. Encircle the correctly spelled words from the following.

	A	B	C
(i)	Fanny	Funny	Funnie
(ii)	Queit	Kweit	Quiet
(iii)	Mischief	Mischef	Misschief
(iv)	Everybudy	Everybody	Everybodi
(v)	Agree	Agrie	Agrea

6. Complete the labelling using a, e, i, o and u.

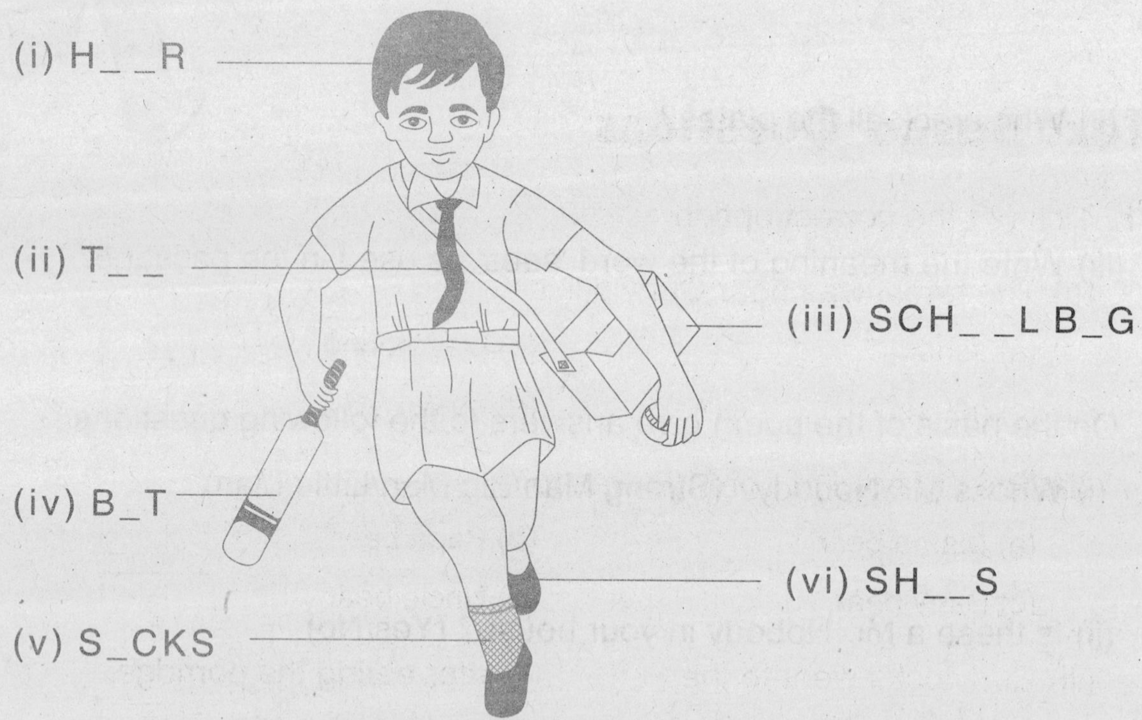

02

Curlylocks and the Three Bears

Text Based Questions

1. Tick (✓) the correct option.

(i) The forest was near Curlylock's ________ .

(a) school ☐ (b) playground ☐

(c) house ☐ (d) hostel ☐

(ii) The big bowl of porridge was for ________ .

(a) Mama bear ☐ (b) Papa bear ☐

(c) Baby bear ☐ (d) Uncle bear ☐

(iii) Curlylocks went to the ________ after eating the porridge.

(a) dining room ☐ (b) store room ☐

(c) study room ☐ (d) bedroom ☐

(iv) There were ________ beds in the bedroom.

(a) three ☐ (b) two ☐

(c) four ☐ (d) five ☐

2. State 'T' for True and 'F' for False statements.

(i) Curlylocks went into the forest at night. ☐

(ii) There was a cottage in the forest. ☐

(iii) The sheep family lived in the cottage. ☐

(iv) The porridge in the middle size bowl was too hot. ☐

3. Read the lines from the story and answer the questions.

Curlylocks was hungry. She ate the porridge from the big bowl. It was very hot.

(i) Who was hungry?

____

(ii) What was very hot?

____

(iii) Write the opposite word of 'hot'.

____

4. On the basis of the chapter give answers to the following questions.

(i) Who lived in the cottage in the forest? (Lion/Bear/Tiger)

____

(ii) Where did Curlylocks go? (School/Cottage/Forest)

____

(iii) What did Curlylocks see on the table? (Bread/Porridge/Fruits)

____

(iv) Which bed was very hard? (Big/Small/Tiny)

____

Language Based Questions

5. Write the plural of the following words.

(i) Bowl ____________ (ii) House ____________

(iii) Table ____________ (iv) Family ____________

(v) Bed ____________ (vi) Cottage ____________

6. Match the following words in Column A with their opposites in Column B.

	Column A		Column B
(i)	Curly	(a)	Up
(ii)	Near	(b)	Straight
(iii)	Cold	(c)	Out
(iv)	Hard	(d)	Far
(v)	In	(e)	Hot
(vi)	Down	(f)	Soft

Unit 7

01 On My Blackboard I can Draw

1. Tick (✓) the correct option.

(i) The child has ________ a little house on the blackboard.

(a) draw ☐ (b) drawn ☐

(c) drawing ☐ (d) draws ☐

(ii) There are four ________ in the house.

(a) doors ☐ (b) windows ☐

(c) chimneys ☐ (d) steps ☐

(iii) The door of the house is coloured ________ .

(a) yellow ☐ (b) brown ☐

(c) red ☐ (d) green ☐

2. State 'T' for True and 'F' for False statements.

(i) The child has drawn a car on the blackboard. ☐

(ii) There are two brown gates in the house. ☐

(iii) The steps are coloured green.

(iv) There are five windows in the house.

(v) Six yellow roses are standing against the wall.

3. Fill in the blanks with suitable words given in the help box.

green, painted, gates, can, little, wide

On my blackboard I (i) ______ draw, One (ii) ______ house with one (iii) ______door, Two brown (iv) ______ that open (v) ______, Four little chimneys (vi) ______white.

4. Read the lines from the poem and answer the questions.

On my blackboard I can draw,
One little house with one green door,

(i) Who is 'I' in the above lines?

____

(ii) What can child draw?

____

(iii) Write the meaning of the word 'little'.

____

5. On the basis of the poem give answers to the following questions.

(i) How do the gates in the house open? (Inside/Wide)

____

(ii) How many windows are shining bright? (Five/Three)

____

(iii) What is the boy doing? (Colour/Draw)

____

(iv) How many marigolds are against the wall? (Five/Six)

____

(v) How many house are there in the poem? (Two/One)

____

Language Based Questions

6. Match the words in Column A with their colours in Column B.

Column A	Column B
(i) Door	(a) Yellow
(ii) Gates	(b) Red
(iii) Chimneys	(c) Brown
(iv) Steps	(d) White
(v) Marigolds	(e) Green

02

Make it Shorter

1. Tick (✓) the correct option.

(i) A _______ was drawn by Akbar.

(a) cycle ☐ (b) pencil ☐

(c) pen ☐ (d) line ☐

(ii) Birbal drew a _______ line.

(a) long ☐ (b) longest ☐

(c) longer ☐ (d) longing ☐

(iii) Everyone in the _______ saw what Birbal drew.

(a) court ☐ (b) courtyard ☐

(c) cottage ☐ (d) cot ☐

2. State 'T' for True and 'F' for False statements.

(i) Akbar drew a line on the wall. ☐

(ii) Akbar ordered to make the line shorter. ☐

(iii) Each minister knew how to make the line shorter. ☐

(iv) Birbal started smiling. ☐

(v) Nobody could make the line shorter. ☐

3. Read the lines from the story and answer the questions that follow.

Birbal drew a longer line under the first one. He didn't touch the first line.

(i) Who draw a longer line?

____

(ii) Which line he didn't touch?

____

(iii) Write the rhyming word of 'longer'.

____

4. On the basis of the chapter give answers to the following questions.

(i) Who draw a line on the floor? (Akbar/Birbal/Minister)

____

(ii) Which line is shorter now? (First/Second)

____

(iii) Who started smiling? (Birbal/Akbar)

____

(iv) Which line he didn't touch? (First/Second)

____

(v) Who was puzzled? (Akbar/Birbal/Minister)

____

Language Based Questions

5. Encircle the words which are spelled correctly.

	A	B	C
(i)	Floar	Floor	Florr
(ii)	Minister	Ministar	Minnister
(iii)	Puggled	Puzled	Puzzled

6. Complete the series.

(i) Heavy, Heavier, __________

(ii) Strong, __________ , Strongest

(iii) Hot, __________ , Hottest

(iv) Good, Better, __________

(v) Bright, Brighter, __________

(vi) Polite, More Polite, __________

7. Identify the following pictures and write their plurals in the given space.

(i)

(ii)

(iii)

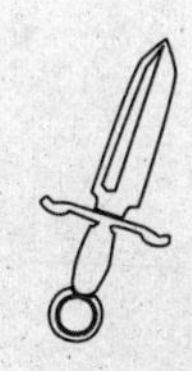

(iv)

(v)

(vi)

(i) ______________________

(ii) ______________________

(iii) ______________________

(iv) ______________________

(v) ______________________

(vi) ______________________

01

I am the Music Man

Text Based Questions

1. Tick (✓) the correct option.

(i) The music man says that he can ________ .

(a) pay ☐ (b) play ☐

(c) say ☐ (d) sway ☐

(ii) The drum which is played by music man is ________ .

(a) thick ☐ (b) heavy ☐

(c) light ☐ (d) big ☐

(iii) The music man can play ________ instruments.

(a) one ☐ (b) three ☐

(c) two ☐ (d) four ☐

2. State 'T' for True and 'F' for False statements.

(i) The poem is about a music girl. ☐

(ii) The music man comes from far away. ☐

(iii) The music man plays the guitar. ☐

(iv) The piano sounds like boomdi, boomdi, boomdi boom. ☐

3. Read the following lines from the poem and answer the questions that follow.

I come from far away,
And I can play

(i) Who is 'I' in the above lines?

____

(ii) Write the rhyming word of 'play'.

____

(iii) Write the opposite of 'far'.

____

Language Based Questions

4. Write the name of the following musical instruments.

(i) (ii) (iii)

(i) _______________ (ii) _______________

(iii) _______________

02

The Mumbai Musicians

1. Tick (✓) the correct option.

(i) The farmer wanted Goopu to see the ________ .

(a) city ☐ (b) country ☐

(c) movie ☐ (d) world ☐

(ii) Goopu wanted to become a ________ .

(a) artist ☐ (b) painter ☐

(c) musician ☐ (d) doctor ☐

(iii) The road to Mumbai was ________ .

(a) clean ☐ (b) dusty ☐

(c) crowded ☐ (d) empty ☐

2. State 'T' for True and 'F' for False statements.

(i) Goopu is the name of a donkey. ☐

(ii) Goopu worked in the house of a merchant. ☐

(iii) Goopu set off towards the city of Delhi. ☐

3. Read the following lines and answer the questions that follow.

They sang. The people inside thought that ghosts had come to scare them.

(i) Who are 'they' in the above lines?

____

(ii) What did the people inside thought?

____

(iii) Write the opposite of the word 'inside'.

____

4. On the basis of the chapter give answers to the following questions.

(i) Who was Goopu? (Donkey/Farmer)

____

(ii) What did the farmer give to Goopu? (Sack of Corn/Grass)

____

(iii) Who was Doopu and Furry? (Dog and Cat/Cock and Deer)

____

(iv) Where did Goopu and Doopu meet Furry? (Road/Mumbai)

____

(v) Who was Furry? (Dog/Cat/Dunkey)

____

(vi) What did Goopu, Doopu and Furry do in the house?
(Ate the Food/Sang)

____

Language Based Questions

5. Name the following animals and write the order in which they met Goopu in the story.

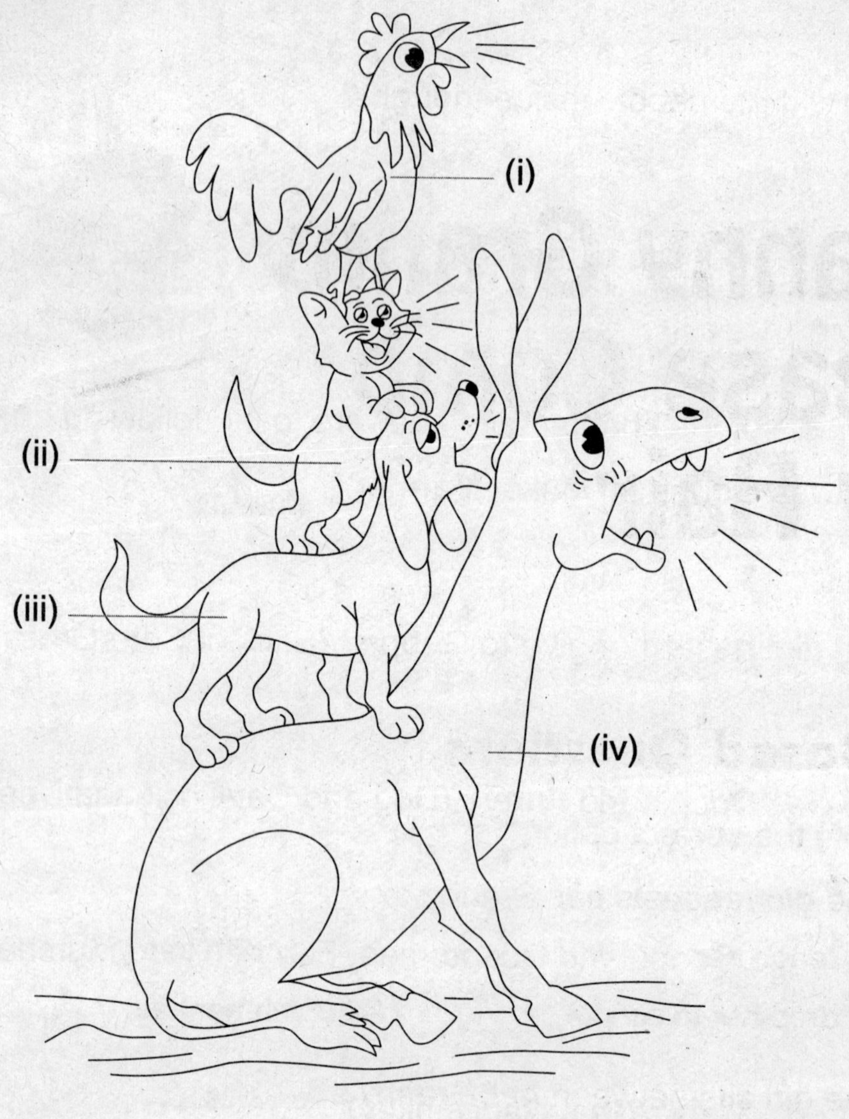

(i) ____________________ (ii) ____________________

(iii) ____________________ (iv) ____________________

01

Granny Granny Please Comb my Hair

Text Based Questions

1. Tick (✓) the correct option.

(i) The girl requests her Granny to ________ .

(a) teach her ☐ (b) play with her ☐

(c) drop her to school ☐ (d) comb her hair ☐

(ii) The girl sits between her Granny's ________ .

(a) arms ☐ (b) thighs ☐

(c) knees ☐ (d) legs ☐

(iii) The Granny always takes her ________ and care for her granddaughter.

(a) clothes ☐ (b) comb ☐

(c) time ☐ (d) effort ☐

2. State 'T' for True and 'F' for False statements.

(i) The girl combs the hair of her grandmother. ☐

(ii) The Granny takes care of her granddaughter. ☐

(iii) The girl sits on a small table. ☐

3. Read the following lines from the poem and answer the questions that follow.

And when you're finished
You always turn my head and say,
"Now, who's a nice girl?"

(i) Who is 'you' in the above lines?

____

(ii) Write the meaning of the word 'nice'.

____

(iii) Write the meaning of the word 'finished'.

____

4. On the basis of the poem give answers to the following questions.

(i) What does the girl ask her Granny to do? (Comb my Hair/Tell a Story)

____

(ii) What does Granny rub on the girl's hair? (Almond Oil/Coconut Oil)

____

(iii) Where does the girl sit? (Cushion/Chair)

____

(iv) Have you ever gone out with your grandparents? (Yes/No)

____

Language Based Questions

5. Encircle the words which are correctly spelled.

	A	B	C
(i)	Cokonut	Cocoanut	Coconut
(ii)	Breeze	Breaze	Breez
(iii)	Cushon	Cushion	Cushen
(iv)	Betwean	Betwiin	Between
(v)	Kneas	Knees	Kneass

6. Write the opposite genders of the following.

(i) Son ______________ (ii) Grandmother ______________

(iii) Uncle ______________ (iv) Sister ______________

(v) Mother ______________ (vi) Boy ______________

7. Write one word in each box that rhymes with the one mentioned in it.

(i) ______ Care (ii) ______ Comb (iii) ______ Oil (iv) ______ Turn

02

The Magic Porridge Pot

Text Based Questions

1. Tick (✓) the correct option.

(i) Tara lived with her ________ .

(a) father ☐ (b) sister ☐

(c) brother ☐ (d) mother ☐

(ii) When Tara said 'Cook-Pot-Cook', the pot ________ .

(a) stopped cooking porridge ☐

(b) started cooking porridge ☐

(c) started making tea ☐

(d) stopped making tea ☐

(iii) Her mother felt ______ when Tara had gone out one day.

(a) angry ☐ (b) hungry ☐

(c) sad ☐ (d) happy ☐

2. State 'T' for True and 'F' for False statements.

(i) Tara was very poor.

(ii) Tara met an old man in the city.

(iii) The old woman gave her a magic pot.

3. On the basis of the chapter give answers to the following questions.

(i) Who was Tara? (Little Girl/Woman)

____

(ii) Where did Tara meet the old woman? (Market/Forest)

____

(iii) What did the old woman give to Tara? (Pot/Money)

____

(iv) With whom did she live? (Mother/Father)

____

(v) What did the magic pot cook? (Tea/Porridge)

____

(vi) Who said, "Do not cook Pot?" (Mother/Old Woman)

____

Language Based Questions

4. The following words are taken from the story and are jumbled. Rearrange them properly.

(i) CGMIA ____________ (ii) ELWOH ____________

(iii) LSPLI ____________ (iv) YPHPA ____________

(v) POTS ____________

5. 'Cooking' is a word from the story that ends with 'ing'. Find two other words from the story that end with 'ing'.

(i) ______________________________

(ii) ______________________________

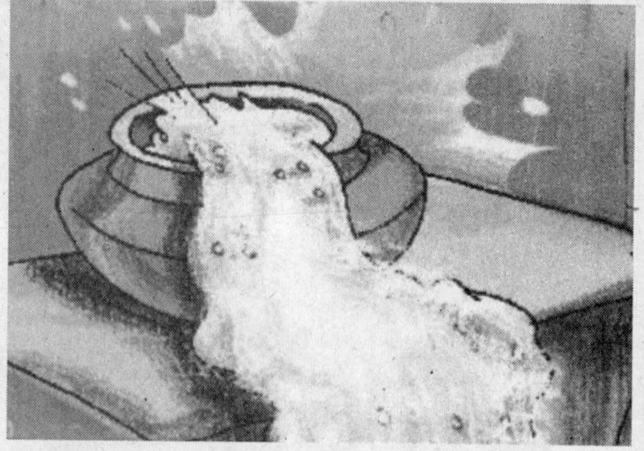

Now, write two more words that end with 'ing'.

(iii) ______________________________

(iv) ______________________________

6. Circle the odd one out from the following pots.

(i)

(ii)

dancing
singing
played
watching

(iii)

(iv)

spoon
pot
bowl
owl

01

Strange Talk

Text Based Questions

1. Tick (✓) the correct option.

(i) The frog did not know how to say ________ .

(a) good night ☐ (b) thank you ☐

(c) good morning ☐ (d) good day ☐

(ii) The duck was asked ________ .

(a) her name ☐ (b) her age ☐

(c) her father's name ☐ (d) how do you do? ☐

(iii) The pups loved to make ________ .

(a) porridge ☐ (b) a row ☐

(c) tea ☐ (d) sandwiches ☐

(iv) There are ________ animals in the poem.

(a) four ☐ (b) three ☐

(c) five ☐ (d) two ☐

2. State 'T' for True and 'F' for False statements.

(i) The little green frog lived above the log.

(ii) The duck said 'Quack-quack'.

(iii) The pig was thin.

(iv) Four pups lived in the kennel.

(v) The pups said 'Bow-wow!' when they wanted to go out.

3. Read the lines given below and answer the questions that follow.

And every time he spoke,
Instead of saying, "Good morning,"
He only said, "Croak-croak."

(i) Who is 'he' in these lines?

(ii) What did 'he' say in place of good morning?

4. On the basis of the poem give answers to the following questions.

(i) Where did the frog live? (Pond/Under a log)

(ii) Where did the duck live? (Waterside/River)

(iii) What did the pig do when asked for dinner? (Croak-croak/Wee-wee)

(iv) Who lived in the kennel? (Pups/Pig)

(v) What are the sounds made by the duck? (Quack-quack/Bow-wow)

____

(vi) What noise do the pups make? (Bow-wow/Wee-wee)

____

(vii) Where did the pigs live? (Sty/Waterside)

____

Language Based Questions

5. Encircle the words which are correctly spelled.

	A	B	C
(i)	Insted	Instaed	Instead
(ii)	Leck	Lack	Leak
(iii)	Waterside	Watarside	Watterside
(iv)	Kennal	Kennel	Keneal
(v)	Dinner	Dinnar	Dinear

6. Write the opposites of the words.

(i) Morning _______________

(ii) Fat _______________

(iii) Good _______________

(iv) Little _______________

(v) Out _______________

(vi) Strange _______________

02

The Grasshopper and the Ant

Text Based Questions

1. Tick (✓) the correct option.

(i) The grasshopper did not like to ________ .

(a) play ☐ (b) sing ☐
(c) laugh ☐ (d) work ☐

(ii) The ants were ________ .

(a) lazy ☐ (b) crazy ☐
(c) hardworking ☐ (d) very lazy ☐

(iii) When the winter came, the grasshopper decided to meet ________

(a) the ants ☐ (b) his friends ☐
(c) his parents ☐ (d) the cockroach ☐

2. Read the following line from the story and answer the questions that follow.

He knocked at her door.

(i) Who is 'He' in the above line?

___

(ii) Who is 'her' in the above line?

___

3. On the basis of the chapter give answers to the following questions.

(i) Who laughed louder? (Grasshopper/Ant)

___

(ii) Who said, "I am hungry and cold?" (Ant/Grasshopper)

___

(iii) What were the ants doing in summer? (Storing Grain/Dance)

___

(iv) Did the grasshopper find food in winter? (Yes/No)

___

(v) Who were singing and dancing in summer? (Ant/Grasshopper)

___

Language Based Questions

4. Circle the odd one out.

(i) Grass, Leaves, Flowers, House

(ii) Ant, Grasshopper, Lion, Fly

(iii) Door, Grain, Window, Chimney

(iv) Sun, Summer, Winter, Autumn

(v) Sun, Moon, Stars, Water

5. Write the names of the following and mention the plural form.

(i) 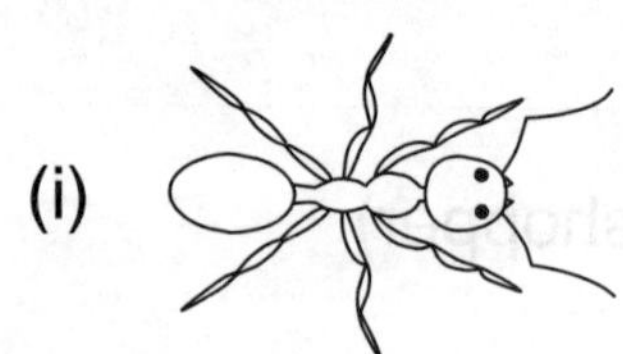

Name ______________________

Plural ______________________

(ii) 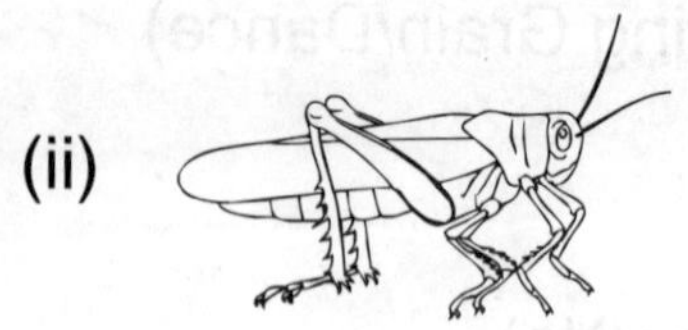

Name ______________________

Plural ______________________

(iii) 

Name ______________________

Plural ______________________

(iv) 

Name ______________________

Plural ______________________

Grammar

01

Vowels and Consonants

There are two kinds of alphabet in English language. These are Vowels and Consonants.

a, e, i, o, u are called Vowels.

All the other alphabets (b c d f g h j k l m n p q r s t v w x y z) are Consonants.

Exercise

1. Look at the **FIRST** letter in these words. Write **V** for Vowel or **C** for Consonant in the box.

(i) The	☐	(ii) End	☐
(iii) Get	☐	(iv) Up	☐
(v) Big	☐	(vi) And	☐
(vii) You	☐	(viii) Who	☐
(ix) In	☐	(x) Want	☐

2. Fill in the blanks with the correct vowel and complete the name of picture given.

(i) 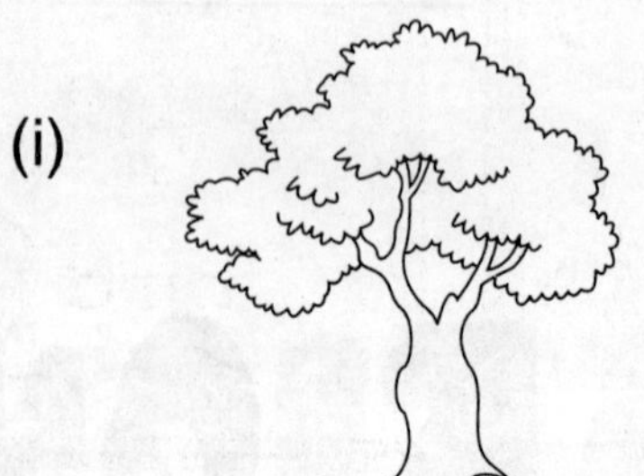 TR __ E

(ii)  C__R

(iii)  ST__R

(iv)  C__T

(v)  S__N

(vi) 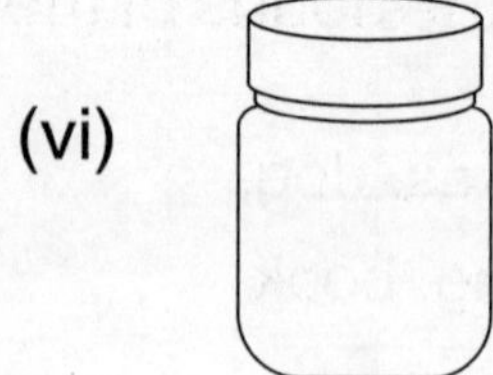 B__TTL__

02

Nouns

Nouns are naming words that tell us about people, places, animals or things.

For example

1. Ashish is a class 2nd student.
2. Delhi is a big city.

In the above sentences, Ashish and Delhi are Nouns.

Meesha, Mrs Jones, Peacock, the Sun, House, Star, Ice-cream, Dog etc are all examples of nouns.

Exercise I

1. Given below in a box are some words. Select the appropriate noun to fill in the blanks and complete the sentence. Also circle the nouns of the box.

Eating, Log, Red, blanket, Robin, lamp, Want, snakes, dog, Tree, Help, Pizza, Sun, Mrs Simpson, dolls, Running, book

(i) The ______________ keeps me warm.

(ii) The ______________ is shining very brightly.

(iii) His pet _______________ scares me.

(iv) _______________ is my favourite food.

(v) My father switched on the _______________ as it was very dark.

(vi) _______________ is my best friend.

(vii) My sister is afraid of _______________ .

(viii) My class-teacher _______________ is very fond of me.

(ix) I finished reading my _______________ .

(x) Sheena loves playing with _______________ .

2. All the words, except one, are nouns. Pick out the word which is not a noun.

(i) Buffalo, Goat, Cow, Black, Horse _______________

(ii) Tea, Milk, Juice, Water, Eat _______________

(iii) Mom, Father, Uncle, With, Aunt _______________

(iv) New Delhi, London, Walk, New York, Australia _______________

(v) Tuesday, On, January, Friday, Sunday _______________

(vi) Gold, Silver, Iron, My, Copper _______________

(vii) Bus, Car, Ship, Aeroplane, Simply _______________

(viii) Apple, Guava, Grape, Through, Mango _______________

(ix) Mountain, Hill, Earth, River, Sleeping _______________

(x) Babies, The, Children, Mothers, Fathers _______________

Exercise II

Nouns can be in singular as well as plural forms. When there are more than one object we use the plural form of that noun. Bananas, Flowers, trucks all have 's' added to the word. But some plural words do not change even in plural form such as sheep.

3. Write the appropriate singular or plural words to match the pictures. Words are given in a box. Write (S) for singular and (P) for plural. One solved example is given for you.

Bug, Kids, Bugs, Dog, Kid, Dogs, Truck, Brush, Trucks, Brushes

Example

4. Choose the correct answer from the given options, for the plural forms of the given words.

(i) Hero

(a) Heros (b) Hero (c) Hires (d) Heroes

(ii) Dictionary

(a) Dictionaris (b) Dictionaries (c) Dictionarys (d) Dictionareis

(iii) Mouse

(a) Mices (b) Mouses (c) Mice (d) Mouse

(iv) Cattle

(a) Cattles (b) Cattle (c) Cats (d) Catles

(v) Leaf

(a) Leafs (b) Lives (c) Leaves (d) Leaf

Exercise III

The gender of a noun tells us whether the noun is a male, female or common. For example father is male, mother is female and parent can be either father or mother or both.

5. Match the masculine gender of nouns of List A with feminine gender of List B.

	List A		List B
(i)	Groom	(a)	Tigress
(ii)	Bull	(b)	Duck
(iii)	Drake	(c)	Bride
(iv)	Gentleman	(d)	Cow
(v)	Lion	(e)	Niece
(vi)	Nephew	(f)	Hen
(vii)	Rooster	(g)	Lady
(viii)	Tiger	(h)	Lioness

6. Rewrite the following sentences after changing the words in bold letters from masculine to feminine as shown in the example.

Example The **King** loved the **prince** very much.

The **Queen** loved the **princess** very much.

(i) My **uncle** has two **sons**.

____

(ii) The **boy** helped the **old man** to cross the street.

____

(iii) My **uncle** and **brother** are going to the cinema tonight.

____

(iv) My **father** invited his friend's family to dinner.

____

(v) We saw a **lion** and a **tiger** at the zoo.

____

Exercise IV

Nouns can also be categorised as Countable or Uncountable Nouns.

Some nouns such as monkey, cat, spoon can be counted and are called as Countable Nouns. But some other nouns such as salt, leaves or water cannot be counted. So, they are called Uncountable Nouns.

7. Some groups of nouns are given below. One is different from the others. It can be countable or uncountable nouns. Tick the odd one from the given options and state whether it is countable or uncountable.

(i) (a) Chair (b) Desk (c) Water (d) Blackboard

(ii) (a) Bread (b) Butter (c) Sugar (d) Apple

(iii) (a) Boys (b) Girls (c) Dust (d) Ladies

(iv) (a) Bicycle (b) Ink (c) Toy train (d) Books

(v) (a) Handbags (b) Shoes (c) Socks (d) Rice

8. Given below are some sentences with nouns. Decide whether these nouns are countable or uncountable nouns. Write (U) for Uncountable and (C) for Countable.

(i) The **children** are playing in the garden. ☐

(ii) I prefer **milk** to **tea**. ☐

(iii) My brother presented me a **cycle**. ☐

(iv) There are a lot of **windows** in our office. ☐

(v) We need to fix this vase with the help of some **glue**. ☐

(vi) My father drinks two **glasses** of water every morning. ☐

(vii) The **food** prepared by my mother is very delicious. ☐

(viii) Some **policemen** are on duty even on Sundays. ☐

(ix) The teacher gave us three **pencils**. ☐

(x) **Exercise** is good for our body. ☐

03

Verbs

Exercise

1. See the pictures below. The incomplete sentences are to be completed with a suitable verb. Choose from the given options.

(i) I ________ with my dog.

(a) feed ☐ (b) play ☐ (c) wash ☐

(ii) The girl can ________ fast.

(a) run ☐ (b) jump ☐ (c) walk 

(iii) Milka is ________ over the wall.

(a) jogging ☐ (b) walking ☐ (c) jumping ☐

(iv) Mary ________ very fast.

(a) walks ☐ (b) sleeps ☐ (c) stands ☐

(v) A girl and a boy are ________ in the room.

(a) playing ☐ (b) dancing ☐ (c) fighting ☐

2. Tick (✓) the correct action words to fill in the given blanks.

(i) Birds ________ in the sky.

(a) fly ☐ (b) dance ☐ (c) cry ☐

(iii) Manjari ________ a glass of juice daily.

(a) eats ☐ (b) drinks ☐ (c) buys ☐

(iii) Reena can ________ in any competition.

(a) read ☐ (b) sing ☐ (c) eat ☐

04

Articles

An **Article** is a word that is used before a noun to point out whether the noun refers to something specific or not. A, An and The are three articles which are used in the English language.

Exercise

1. Given below are words used with Articles A, An, The. Tick (✓) the word which does not have a correct article.

(i) (a) An umbrella ☐ (b) A egg ☐

(c) The owl ☐ (d) An oven ☐

(ii) (a) A Sun ☐ (b) The Taj Mahal ☐

(c) An elephant ☐ (d) A bird ☐

(iii) (a) An Eiffel Tower ☐ (b) An old man ☐

(c) A tree ☐ (d) A bicycle ☐

(iv) (a) A Ganga ☐ (b) The house ☐

(c) An apple ☐ (d) An ice-cream ☐

(v) (a) An inkpot ☐ (b) A banana ☐

(c) The horse ☐ (d) A nurse ☐

2. A few sentences are given below with some articles. State whether the articles in the sentences are used correctly or not.

(i) **An** umbrella is **an** useful thing. ☐

(ii) I met **a** ugly woman in **an** street. ☐

(iii) He is **the** honest man. ☐

(iv) **The** clock is not working properly. ☐

(v) **The** Church is lively on Sundays. ☐

3. Use 'a' or 'an' before these words.

(i) __________ orange (ii) __________ doctor

(iii) __________ elephant (iv) __________ inkpot

(v) __________ frog (vi) __________ bicycle

(vii) __________ tiger (viii) __________ egg

(ix) __________ umbrella (x) __________ book

05

Pronouns

Pronouns are the words used in place of Nouns.

Example

Rita is a good girl. I like **Rita**.

Instead of using nouns at both places in the above sentence we can use a pronoun. So, the sentence will become

Rita is a good girl. I like **her**.

Here '**her**' is a pronoun used for Rita.

Some commonly used pronouns are

I, you, he, she, we, they, me, him, her, us, them, mine, yours,his, our, their etc

Exercise

1. Choose the correct answer from the given options.

(i) My grandmother presented this watch to ________ .

(a) I ☐ (b) mine ☐

(c) me ☐ (d) myself ☐

(ii) I love my dog. I take _______ for a walk everyday.

(a) it ☐ (b) I ☐

(c) itself ☐ (d) myself ☐

(iii) Those apples belong to ________ .

(a) they ☐ (b) theirs ☐

(c) themselves ☐ (d) them ☐

(iv) This watch belongs to my mother. It is ________ .

(a) her ☐ (b) she ☐

(c) hers ☐ (d) herself ☐

(v) Father is giving _______ a bicycle on your birthday.

(a) you ☐ (b) yourself ☐

(c) yours ☐ (d) themselves ☐

2. Use the correct pronoun for the words in bold letters in the sentences and rewrite the sentences.

(i) Mohit is my cousin. I went to the zoo with **Mohit**.

____

(ii) The table in my house is very big. The **table** has a glass top.

____

(iii) I love my parents. My **parents** love me too.

____

(iv) Ramesh is a rich man. **Ramesh** has a very big house.

____

(v) My mother's name is Anita. My **mother** loves me very much.

____

06

Adjectives

As nouns are naming words, adjectives are describing words. They describe more about a noun— For example

1. I live in a **big** house.
2. Sheena is a **talkative** girl.
3. I like **red** apples.

The words big, talkative and red in the above sentences are Adjectives.

Exercise

1. Read the sentences and fill in the blanks with appropriate adjective.

(i) We love eating _______ Snacks on a cold or rainy day.

(a) cold ☐ (b) hot ☐ (c) sturdy ☐

(ii) Some birds have _______ feathers.

(a) bright ☐ (b) colourful ☐ (c) both (a) and (b) ☐

(iii) Shimla is a _______ place.

(a) dry ☐ (b) cold ☐ (c) hot ☐

(iv) My mom made a ______ cake for the party.

(a) delicious ☐ (b) cold ☐ (c) chilly ☐

(v) He has painted his room ______.

(a) oil ☐ (b) blue ☐ (c) tiled ☐

2. Tick (✓) the adjective from each set of words.

(i) (a) Frog ☐ (b) Fix ☐
(c) Run ☐ (d) Large ☐

(ii) (a) Fun ☐ (b) Brick ☐
(c) Beautiful ☐ (d) Turn ☐

(iii) (a) Bake ☐ (b) Lock ☐
(c) Use ☐ (d) Quiet ☐

(iv) (a) Cut ☐ (b) Old ☐
(c) Sleep ☐ (d) Stick ☐

(v) (a) Soap ☐ (b) Kick ☐
(c) Broken ☐ (d) Brother ☐

01

Paragraph Writing

Sample Paragraph

☑ *Write a few lines about your Mother .*

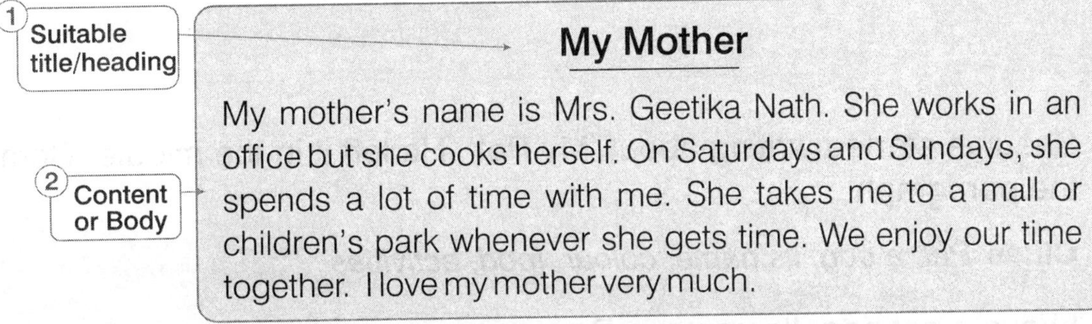

My Mother

My mother's name is Mrs. Geetika Nath. She works in an office but she cooks herself. On Saturdays and Sundays, she spends a lot of time with me. She takes me to a mall or children's park whenever she gets time. We enjoy our time together. I love my mother very much.

PRACTICE QUESTIONS

1. Write a paragraph on Rainy Day. You may use the following clues.

Clues *Raining heavily, water on the road, ground, paper boats, used umbrella/raincoat, to go back home, ate snacks with tea*

Rainy Day

A few days ago ____________________

____

____

____

____

2. Write a few lines about your visit to a zoo with your family last Sunday. You may use the following clues.

Clues *Sunday, a sunny day, went to the zoo with parents, tickets bought, saw many types of birds and animals, enjoyed a lot*

____

____

____

____

3. Shaurya started writing about 'My Pet'. He left it in the middle. Complete the paragraph.

Clues *Pet, a dog, its name, colour, food, activities*

I have a pet dog. Its name is Ron. ____________________

____

____

____

____

02

Picture Comprehension

1. Look at the picture given below and answer the questions that follow. You may take the help of the clues given in the box.

Clues *Diyas, rangoli, burst crackers, Diwali*

(i) What does the picture tell us?

(ii) The picture is taken at the time of

(iii) What is the girl in the picture doing?

2. See the picture and complete the following lines on it using the clues.

Clues *Going to school, schoolbag, flowers, on his back, playing with ball*

(i) A girl and a boy are ______________.

(ii) Another boy and girl are ______________.

(iii) The boy is holding ______________ in one of his hands.

3. See the picture given below and answer the questions that follow. You may take help from the clues.

Clues *Feeding the ducks, a box, on the ground, feeding, scarf*

(i) Where is the girl standing?

____

(ii) What are the ducks doing?

____

(iii) What does the girl have in her right hand?

____

4. Look at the picture and complete the following lines on it using the clues.

Clues *Cock, chicks, morning scene, eating grass, open, ducklings*

(i) The ________________ is sitting on a fence.

(ii) Its mouth is ________________.

(iii) The hens are with their ________________.

(iv) A duck is there with its two ________________.

Answer Sheet

(Section A)

Unit 1

Chapter 1 First Day at School

1. (i) (a) (ii) (b) (iii) (c)

3. (i) Night (ii) Enemy (iii) Empty (iv) Bad (v) Cry

4. (i) Yes (ii) Yes (iii) No (iv) Yes (v) No (vi) Yes

5. (i) Blackboard (ii) Teacher (iii) Students

Chapter 2 Haldi's Adventure

1. (i) (d) (ii) (a) (iii) (c)

2. (i) T (ii) F (iii) F (iv) F (v) F

3. (ii) (e) (iii) (a) (iv) (b) (v) (c)

4. (i) school, day (ii) Mondays, Thursdays, Fridays (iii) play, games, school
(iv) school, giraffe **5.** (iii) Slow

6. (i) Book (ii) Big Glasses (iii) Stars, Trees, Birds, Animals (iv) Saturdays (v) Gone Away

Unit 2

Chapter 1 I am Lucky

1. (i) (c) (ii) (b) **2.** (i) T (ii) F (iii) F (iv) T

3. (i) were (ii) thankful (iii) raise, trunk (iv) kangaroo (v) try (vi) moon

4. (ii) (c) (iii) (a) (iv) (e) (v) (b)

5. (iii) tree **6.** (i) Butterfly, Myna (ii) Fish, Octopus (iii) Myna

7. (i) Thankless (ii) Cry (iii) Unhappiness (iv) Drop

8. (i) Butterflies (ii) Fish or Fishes (iii) Trunks (iv) Moons (v) Octopuses

9. (i) Thankful (ii) Tree (iii) Giggle (iv) Raise (v) Right

Chapter 2 I Want

1. (i) (b) (ii) (c) (iii) (a)

2. (i) T (ii) F (iii) T (iv) F **3.** (iii) listen

4. (i) Wise Woman (ii) Magic Wand (iii) Long Neck
(iv) Zebra (v) Stripes

5. (i) (d) (ii) (e) (iii) (a) (iv) (b) (v) (c)

6. (i) (c) (ii) (b) (iii) (d) (iv) (a) (v) (d)

7. (i) Tiger (ii) Giraffe (iii) Elephant (iv) Zebra

Unit 3

Chapter 1 A Smile

1. (i) (d) (ii) (c) (iii) (b)
2. (i) T (ii) F (iii) F (iv) T (v) F
3. (i) funny (ii) secret (iii) wonderful (iv) smiles
4. (i) WRINKLE (ii) NEVER (iii) SMILE (iv) FUNNY (v) WONDER
5. (i) (c) (ii) (e) (iii) (d) (iv) (a) (v) (b)
6. (i) great (ii) cover up (iii) a long distance (iv) look at

Chapter 2 The Wind and the Sun

1. (i) (c) (ii) (d) (iii) (d)
2. (i) F (ii) T (iii) T (iv) F **3.** (ii) Sun (iii) Hold
4. (i) Road (ii) Sun (iii) Blowing Harder (iv) Hold Tightly (v) Shines Hard (vi) Sun
5. (i) that (ii) away (iii) cannot (iv) turn (v) won
6. (i) Let me try. (ii) Who is stronger? (iii) He shines hard. (iv) I give up.
7. (i) Belt (ii) Jeans (iii) Spectacles (iv) Shirt (v) Shorts (vi) Vest

Unit 4

Chapter 1 Rain

1. (i) (d) (ii) (c) (iii) (c) **2.** (i) F (ii) F (iii) T
3. (i) raining (ii) field (iii) umbrellas (iv) sea **4.** (iii) Yes
5. (i) Field (ii) Ships (iii) Umbrellas
6. (i) Train (ii) Call (iii) Sand (iv) Trip (Your answers can be different)
7. (i) Duck (ii) Engine (iii) Sea (iv) Socks
8. (i) Fields (ii) Trees (iii) Ships (iv) Seas
9. (ii) Sunshine (iii) Moonlight (iv) Cloudburst (v) Weekend (vi) Rainbow
10. (i) It is raining. (ii) Ground is full of water.
    (iii) Small children are sitting or jumping in the water.
    (iv) One girl is standing with an umbrella.
    (v) There are lots of clouds above in the sky.

Chapter 2 Storm in the Garden

1. (i) (d) (ii) (b) (iii) (c) (iv) (a)
2. (i) F (ii) T (iii) T (iv) F **3.** (iii) Suddenly
4. (i) Friends (ii) Ants (iii) Feelers (iv) Snail
5. (i) Push (ii) Dark (iii) Dry (iv) Over
6. (i) Ant (ii) Frog (iii) Snake (iv) Cockroach (v) Ladybird

Unit 5

Chapter 1 Zoo Manners

1. (i) (d) (ii) (b) (iii) (a)
2. (i) T (ii) F (iii) F (iv) F (v) T
3. (i) careful (ii) fun (iii) much (iv) understand (v) well
4. (i) Animals (ii) Do (iii) Alert
5. (i) Hump (ii) Strutting (iii) Yes (iv) Animals, Birds
6. (i) B (ii) A (iii) C (iv) A (v) C
7. (i) Bump (ii) Take (iii) Sell (iv) Beat (Your answers can be different)

Chapter 2 Funny Bunny

1. (i) (c) (ii) (d) (iii) (c)
2. (i) F (ii) T (iii) F (iv) T (v) F
3. (iii) All 4. (i) Tree (ii) Nut (iii) Woxy Foxy (iv) Sky
5. (i) I am (ii) I will (iii) We are
6. (i) (b) (ii) (c) (iii) (d) (iv) (a)
7. (i) Sky (ii) Gate (iii) Ship (iv) Stone
8. (i) Hen (ii) Cock (iii) Rabbit (iv) Duck (v) Goose

Unit 6

Chapter 1 Mr. Nobody

1. (i) (d) (ii) (c) (iii) (b) (iv) (a)
2. (i) funny (ii) quiet (iii) mouse (iv) mischief (v) everybody's
3. (iii) look at 4. (i) Little Man (ii) Yes (Your answers can be different)
   (iii) Mouse (iv) Mouse
5. (i) B (ii) C (iii) A (iv) B (v) A
6. (i) HAIR (ii) TIE (iii) SCHOOLBAG (iv) BAT (v) SOCKS
   (vi) SHOES

Chapter 2 Curlylocks and the Three Bears

1. (i) (c) (ii) (b) (iii) (d) (iv) (a)
2. (i) F (ii) T (iii) F (iv) F
3. (iii) Cold
4. (i) Bear (ii) Forest (iii) Porridge (iv) Big
5. (i) Bowls (ii) Houses (iii) Tables (iv) Families (v) Beds (vi) Cottages
6. (i) (b) (ii) (d) (iii) (e) (iv) (f) (v) (c) (vi) (a)

Unit 7

Chapter 1 On My Blackboard I can Draw

1. (i) (b) (ii) (c) (iii) (d)
2. (i) F (ii) T (iii) F (iv) T (v) F
3. (i) can (ii) little (iii) green (iv) gates (v) wide (vi) painted
4. (iii) Small **5.** (i) Wide (ii) Five (iii) Draw (iv) Six (v) One
6. (i) (e) (ii) (c) (iii) (d) (iv) (b) (v) (a)

Chapter 2 Make it Shorter

1. (i) (d) (ii) (c) (iii) (a)
2. (i) F (ii) T (iii) F (iv) T (v) F **3.** (iii) Under
4. (i) Akbar (ii) First (iii) Birbal (iv) First (v) Minister
5. (i) B (ii) A (iii) C
6. (i) Heaviest (iii) Hotter (iv) Brightest (ii) Stronger (iv) Best (vi) Most Polite
7. (i) Birds (ii) Leaves (iii) Cacti (iv) Knives (v) Kings (vi) Balls

Unit 8

Chapter 1 I am the Music Man

1. (i) (b) (ii) (d) (iii) (c)
2. (i) F (ii) T (iii) F (iv) F
3. (ii) Away (iii) Near **4.** (i) Piano (ii) Drum (iii) Guitar

Chapter 2 The Mumbai Musicians

1. (i) (d) (ii) (c) (iii) (b)
2. (i) T (ii) F (iii) F **3.** (iii) Outside
4. (i) Donkey (ii) Sack of Corn (iii) Dog and Cat (iv) Road
   (v) Cat (vi) Ate the Food
5. (i) Cuckoo (ii) Furry (iii) Doopu (iv) Goopu
   Doopu was the first to meet Goopu, followed by Furry and Cuckoo.

Unit 9

Chapter 1 Granny Granny Please Comb my Hair

1. (i) (d) (ii) (c) (iii) (c) **2.** (i) F (ii) T (iii) F
3. (ii) Good (iii) Completed
4. (i) Comb my Hair (ii) Coconut Oil (iii) Cushion
   (iv) Yes (Your answers can be different)
5. (i) C (ii) A (iii) B (iv) C (v) B
6. (i) Daughter (ii) Grandfather (iii) Aunt (iv) Brother (v) Father (vi) Girl
7. (i) Fare (ii) Tomb (iii) Foil (iv) Burn (Your answers can be different)

Chapter 2 The Magic Porridge Pot

1. (i) (d) (ii) (b) (iii) (b)
2. (i) T (ii) F (iii) T
3. (i) Little Girl (ii) Forest (iii) Pot (iv) Mother (v) Porridge (vi) Mother
4. (i) MAGIC (ii) WHOLE (iii) SPILL (iv) HAPPY (v) STOP
5. (i) Making (ii) Spilling (iii) Studying (iv) Playing
6. (i) ate (ii) played (iii) water (iv) owl

Unit 10

Chapter 1 Strange Talk

1. (i) (c) (ii) (d) (iii) (b) (iv) (a)
2. (i) F (ii) T (iii) F (iv) F (v) T
4. (i) Under a Log (ii) Waterside (iii) Wee-wee (iv) Pups (v) Quack-quack (vi) Bow-wow (vii) Sty
5. (i) C (ii) B (iii) A (iv) B (v) A
6. (i) Evening (ii) Thin (iii) Bad (iv) Large (v) In (vi) Usual

Chapter 2 The Grasshopper and the Ant

1. (i) (d) (ii) (c) (iii) (a)
3. (i) Grasshopper (ii) Grasshopper (iii) Storing Grain (iv) No (v) Grasshopper
4. (i) House (ii) Lion (iii) Grain (iv) Sun (v) Water
5.

Name	Plural
(i) Ant	Ants
(ii) Grasshopper	Grasshoppers
(iii) Fox	Foxes
(iv) Tiger	Tigers

(Section B)

Chapter 1 Vowels and Consonants

1. (i) C (ii) V (iii) C (iv) V (v) C (vi) V (vii) C (viii) C (ix) V (x) C
2. (i) Vowel (E) TREE (ii) Vowel (A) CAR (iii) Vowel (A) STAR (iv) Vowel (A) CAT (v) Vowel (U) SUN (vi) Vowel (O, E) BOTTLE

Chapter 2 Nouns

1. (i) blanket (ii) Sun (iii) dog (iv) Pizza (v) lamp (vi) Robin (vii) snakes (viii) Mrs Simpson (ix) book (x) dolls
2. (i) Black (ii) Eat (iii) With (iv) Walk (v) On (vi) My (vii) Simply (viii) Through (ix) Sleeping (x) The

3. (i) Truck (S) Trucks (P) (ii) Brush (S) Brushes (P) (iii) Kids (P) Kid (S)
(iv) Bug (S) Bugs (P)

4. (i) (d) (ii) (b) (iii) (c) (iv) (b) (v) (c)

5. (i) (c) (ii) (d) (iii) (b) (iv) (g) (v) (h) (vi) (e)
(vii) (f) (viii) (a)

6. (i) aunt, daughters (ii) girl, old woman (iii) aunt, sister
(iv) mother (v) lioness, tigress

7. (i) (c) Uncountable (ii) (d) Countable (iii) (c) Uncountable
(iv) (b) Uncountable (v) (d) Uncountable

8. (i) C (ii) U (iii) C (iv) C (v) U (vi) C
(vii) U (viii) C (ix) C (x) U

Chapter 3 Verbs

1. (i) (b) (ii) (a) (iii) (c) (iv) (a) (v) (b)
2. (i) (a) (ii) (b) (iii) (b)

Chapter 4 Articles

1. (i) (b) (ii) (a) (iii) (a) (iv) (a) (v) (c)
2. (i) **Incorrect** 'an useful thing' should be changed to 'a useful thing'
(ii) **Incorrect** 'a ugly woman' should be changed to 'an ugly woman'
'an street' should be changed to 'a street'
(iii) **Incorrect** 'the honest man' should be changed to 'an honest man'
(iv) Correct (v) Correct
3. (i) an (ii) a (iii) an (iv) an (v) a (vi) a
(vii) a (viii) an (ix) an (x) a

Chapter 5 Pronouns

1. (i) (c) (ii) (a) (iii) (d) (iv) (c) (v) (a)
2. (i) Mohit → him
Mohit is my cousin. I went to the zoo with him.
(ii) Table → It
The table in my house is very big. It has a glass top.
(iii) Parents → They
I love my Parents. They love me too.
(iv) Ramesh → He
Ramesh is a rich man. He has a very big house.
(v) Mother → She
My mother name is Anita. She loves me very much.

Chapter 6 Adjectives

1. (i) (b) (ii) (c) (iii) (b) (iv) (a) (v) (b)
2. (i) (d) (ii) (c) (iii) (d) (iv) (b) (v) (c)